Published By Robert Corbin

@ Leonard Myers

Wheat Belly Diet for Beginners: Easy

Start Tips

All Right RESERVED

ISBN 978-87-94477-34-5

TABLE OF CONTENTS

Cheeseburger Soup 1

Cucumber Salad With Homemade Sour Cream Dill Dressing 4

Colorful Steamed Vegetables 6

Banana Cream Pie 8

Baked Leek, Potato, And Parmesan Frittata 10

Chicken & White Bean Salad 11

Banana & Blueberry Muffins 14

Italian Style Ravioli 17

Spiced Apples 19

Duck In A Date Sauce 20

Pecanencrusted Chicken With Tapenade 24

Crab Cakes 26

Potato Salad With Peas And Green Beans 29

Asparagus And Avocado Salad 31

Goat Cheese And Roast Tomatoes Stuffed Portobello Mushrooms 32

Healthy Gourmet Goulash	35
Magically Wheat Free Cereal	37
Eiffel Tower Toast	39
Toad In A Hole Meat Version	41
Sausage And Ham Roll	43
Pumpkin And Walnut Muffins	45
Blueberry Muffins	46
Peach Coconut Muffins	48
Thai Style Beef Salad	51
Melon Chilled Soup	54
Lemon And Rosemary Teacakes|243 Calories	56
Marzipan Cake|304 Calories	58
Oven Baked Hot Wings	59
Veggie Wheatfree Pasta	62
Almond Strawberry Yogurt	65
Flaxseed Breakfast Wrap	66
Roasted Squash Soup	68
Stuffed Tomatoes	70

Shrimp Skewers 71

Simple Blueberry Pancakes 73

Cod With Herbs 75

Mixed Bean Stew 77

Slow Cooked Chili Con Carne 79

Zucchini With Baby Bella Mushrooms 82

Turkeyavocado Wraps 84

Grilled Pear Salad With Walnut And Pomegranate
   Vinaigrette 86

Creamy Cauliflower Salad 88

Vegetable Stirfry 89

Chicken With Prunes And Green Olives 91

Honeylime Chicken Skewers Key West Style 94

Mushroom Risotto 96

Eggy Booster 99

Delicious Potato And Egg Party 101

Greek Souvlaki 102

Chicken Salad With Peas 104

Irish Soda Bread 106

Chocolate Zucchini Bread 108

Double Chocolate Chunk Cookies 110

Squash Parmesan Cakes 113

Chicken Stuffed Tomatoes 115

Sausage And Mushroom Quiches 116

Shrimp With Curried Rice 119

Apple Cake 122

Pumpkin Pie 124

Wonderful Coconut Shrimp 127

Chicken Cornbread Casserole 129

Simple Pancakes 132

Cream Of Wheat Alternative 134

Chicken Salad 135

Roasted Chicken 137

Oriental Nutty Chicken 139

Nutty Energy Bars 142

Slow Cooked Prawn Curry 144

Oriental Barbecued Pork 146

Cheeseburger Soup

Ingredients:

- 1 Tbsp. parsley
- 1/8 tsp. ground black pepper
- ¼ tsp. paprika
- 1 Tbsp. flour, coconut
- ½ cup sharp cheddar cheese, shredded
- 1 Tbsp. butter, unsalted
- 3 3/4 cups + ¼ cup chicken broth
- ½ head of cauliflower
- 1 yellow onion, diced
- ½ pound lean ground beef
- ½ tsp. salt

Directions:

1. Add 3 ¾ cups of chicken broth into a large pot. Cut the florets from the cauliflower and place them into the pot. Set the pot on the stove over high heat and bring the mixture to a boil.
2. Place the butter into a pan and melt on the stove over mediumhigh heat. Add the onions and sauté for several minutes until tender and golden in color.
3. Add the beef and cook while crumbling the beef up a bit with a spatula.
4. Cook until browned and then drain the grease from the beef. Place the cooked and crumbled beef back into the pan.
5. Stir the parsley, paprika, salt and pepper into the browned beef and cook for 2 minutes. Remove the pan from the heat and set to the side for the moment.

6. Transfer the cauliflower mixture from Step 1 into a food processor and blend until smooth. Place the smoothed mixture back into the pot.
7. In a small bowl, whisk the remaining ¼ cup of chicken broth with the coconut flour until smooth.
8. Add this to the smoothed cauliflower mixture from Step 4 and stir. Set the pot on the stove and cook for 5 minutes while whisking.
9. Transfer the soup into serving bowls and enjoy.

Cucumber Salad With Homemade Sour Cream Dill Dressing

Ingredients:

- 6 cucumbers, sliced thinly
- Coarse salt, to taste
- Ground black pepper, to taste
- ½ cup sour cream, reducedfat
- 2 Tbsp. fresh dill, chopped
- 2 Tbsp. lemon juice

Directions:

1. In a mixing bowl, whisk together the sour cream, dill and lemon juice. Season the mixture with black pepper and salt.
2. Add the cucumbers to the sour cream mixture and toss until well coated.

3. Consume the salad immediately or transfer into a container with a lid and refrigerate until ready.

Colorful Steamed Vegetables

Ingredients:

- 1 red bell pepper, cut into ½inch wide strips
- 2 medium carrots, peeled and shredded
- 2 tablespoons fatfree chicken broth
- 1 tablespoon lowfat Parmesan cheese
- Head of broccoli, cut into florets
- 6 large zucchini, cut as shown
- 4 large yellow squash, cut diagonally into ¾inch wide slices

Directions:

1. Place vegetables in a large microwaveable covered dish.
2. Pour chicken broth over vegetables.

3. Microwave, covered, on highpower until tender but not soft, about five to ten minutes.
4. Leave covered for 2 minutes.
5. Season with Parmesan cheese and salt.

Banana Cream Pie

Ingredients:

- 2 ripe bananas
- 3 tablespoons cornstarch
- 1 tablespoon banana flavor extract
- 1 tablespoon vanilla extract
- 3 lowfat graham crackers
- 2 cups 1% fat milk
- ¾ cup Sweet
- ½ cup fatfree sour cream
- Half (7ounce) can fatfree Reddiwip

Directions:

1. In a large saucepan, whisk together milk, Sweet, starch, banana extract, and vanilla extract.
2. Cook over mediumhigh heat, stirring frequently, until the mixture thickens and begins to boil. Transfer to a medium mixing bowl and allow cooling to room temperature.
3. Arrange graham crackers in a 9inch glass pie plate.
4. Fold sour cream and Reddiwip into the thickened milk mixture.
5. Peel and cut bananas into ¼inch slices. Arrange slices on top of graham crackers.
6. Turn filling out over bananas and spread evenly.

Baked Leek, Potato, And Parmesan Frittata

Ingredients:

- 1 garlic cloves, minced
- ½ pound potatoes cut in cubes
- 5 large eggs
- ½ tsp. chilli powder
- ½ cup ricotta cheese
- ¼ teaspoon olive oil
- ½ cup water
- 2 bunch leeks sliced in small pieces
- 1/2 cup Parmesan cheese

Directions:

1. Preheat oven to 375o F. Brush a square baking pan 9 inches with oil.

2. Boil water in a medium saucepan over high heat. Add the leeks, garlic and potatoes; Season with salt.
3. Reduce heat to mediumlow and cook, covered, until the potatoes are tender, about 10 minutes. Let cool down.
4. Beat 1 egg white, 1/2 teaspoon salt and chilli powder. Add the potato mixture and ricotta. Mix 1/4 cup of the Parmesan. Pour in pan and sprinkle with the remaining Parmesan.
5. Bake until the edges are set, about 12 minutes.
6. Reduce the oven temperature to 325 degrees and bake until it is firm about 25 minutes. Let cool for 10 minutes. Take out and cut into 8 parts and serve.

Chicken & White Bean Salad

Ingredients:

Vinaigrette

- 5 tablespoons olive oil
- 6 tablespoons fresh orange juice
- ¼ cup whitewine vinegar
- 1 tablespoon mustard
- 1 clove garlic
- Salt to taste

Salad

- 1 ½ cups diced celery
- ¼ cup feta cheese
- 1 cup fresh basil
- Salt, pepper to taste
- 2 cups romaine lettuce
- 1 can beans (white)

- 2 ½ cups diced cooked chicken breast
- 2 cups diced zucchini

Directions:

To Prepare The Vinaigrette:

1. Mash Garlic and some olive oil in a thick paste.
2. Mix in remaining oil. Add orange juice, vinegar and mustard; beat until smooth.
3. Season with salt, if desired. Set aside at room temperature.

To Prepare The Salad:

1. Combine the beans, chicken, zucchini, celery, cheese in a large bowl and mix well. Add the chopped basil and dressing.

Banana & Blueberry Muffins

Ingredients:

- 1 egg
- ¼ cup wheat germ
- 1 tsp baking powder
- ¾ cup whole wheat flour
- ½ cup chopped walnuts
- 1 tsp baking soda
- ¼ tsp salt
- 1 cup blueberries
- ¾ cup allpurpose flour
- 1 tbsp sunflower oil
- ¼ cup oat bran
- ¼ cup quick cooking oats

- ¾ cup white sugar

- 1 banana, mashed

- 1 cup buttermilk

Directions:

2. Preheat the oven to 350F.
3. Using lowcalorie cooking spray grease a 12piece muffin tray or prepare a muffin tray with muffin cups.
4. Combine both types of flour, oats, wheat germ, bran, baking soda and baking powder with a pinch of salt.
5. Add the walnuts and blueberries next, stirring to ensure an even distribution.
6. In a different mixing bowl, add together the rest of the remaining Ingredients:. Stir or blend to produce a thick but smooth mixture.
7. Incorporate the dry mixture into the wet mixture. Beat thoroughly until everything has mixed together and there are no lumps.

8. Distribute the muffin batter evenly between the 12 cups with a spoon; there should be enough batter for each muffin cup or hole to be full.
9. Bake for 17 minutes or until the muffins are golden brown and slightly springy.

Italian Style Ravioli

Ingredients:

- 4 tbsp olive oil
- 1 onion, chopped into eight pieces
- 2 teaspoons dried oregano
- ½ cup grated Parmesan cheese
- 1 lb ditalini pasta
- 1*14oz canned cannellini beans, rinsed & drains
- 1 tbsp dried parsley
- 2 teaspoons dried basil
- 2 cloves garlic, minced
- 2*14oz canned chopped tomatoes
- 6 cups water

- 1*14oz canned navy beans, rinsed & drained

Directions:

1. In a large saucepan, warm olive oil over a high heat. Toss in the onion and cook for 57 minutes, or until the onion has softened and browned.
2. Lower the heat and toss in the remaining Ingredients:, except for the pasta. Cover and leave to simmer for 60 minutes.
3. In a different saucepan, bring water to the boil.
4. Add a pinch of salt and the pasta. Cook for 10 minutes, then remove.
5. Add a portion of sauce to the pasta and serve immediately.

Spiced Apples

Ingredients:

- 2 tablespoons of raisins
- ¾ teaspoon of ground ginger
- 80ml water
- A dash of cream
- 4 red apples
- 80g brown sugar
- 45g unsalted butter
- 2 tablespoons of pecans, finely chopped

Directions:

1. Core the apples using an apple corer, ensuring that the bottom of the apple remains attached.

2. With a spoon pry away some more of the apple flesh so there is a sizable hole in the middle of each apple
3. . Using a sharp knife, score the skin of each apple several times.
4. Chop the pecans and the raisins into small pieces. Add the pecans, sugar, butter, raisins and ginger into a mixing bowl and stir.
5. Divide this mixture into four portions and fill the space created in the apples with this mixture.
6. Place your apples in your slow cooker. Add enough water to the slow cooker so that your apples are almost, but not entirely, submerged.
7. Bake on a high temperature for 2 hours and 30 minutes. Serve each apple with a dash of cream.

Duck In A Date Sauce

Ingredients:

- 2 teaspoons sunflower oil
- 1 tablespoon of cinnamon
- 1 teaspoon of ground ginger
- 2 lemons
- 200g dates
- 400ml passata
- 100g almonds
- Fresh mint
- 6 duck legs (skinned)
- 2 garlic cloves
- 1 red chili
- 2 inch ginger stem
- 1 tablespoon of cumin

- 1 tablespoon of coriander

Directions:

1. In a frying pan, warm the sunflower oil and fry the dugs legs until golden brown all over, one at a time.
2. Next, turn your slow cooker to a low heat and place the duck legs within.
3. Dice the onion. Cut the lemons into halves, removing the pulp and pith. Using a food processor, blend the onion, garlic, chili, ginger and the lemon skin into a paste.
4. Next, in the frying pan that was used to brown the duck legs, fry the paste for 5 minutes or until soft. Remove and set aside.
5. Place the dates into the food processor with 1 cup of water. Process until another paste is formed.
6. Scoop the date paste into the slow cooker with the duck legs and pour in the lemon seasoning.

7. Finally, pour the peseta into the slow cooker and stir thoroughly. Slow cook the duck legs in sauce for at least 5 hours.
8. Garnish with chopped almonds and serve with a side of your choice.

Pecanencrusted Chicken With Tapenade

Ingredients:

- 2 piece boneless and skinless chicken breasts
- 1 teaspoon dried oregano
- 1 large egg
- ½cup ground pecans
- ¼cup coconut milk or dairy milk
- Fine sea salt and ground black pepper
- 4 tablespoons storebought caponata, tapenade, or pesto
- 3 tablespoons grated Parmesan cheese
- 2 teaspoons onion powder

Directions:

1. Preheat the oven to 175°C. Put in the chicken until it's baked for about 30 minutes.
2. Crack 1 egg and beat it lightly using the fork in a bowl.
3. Add in the milk with the egg. Mix together and then add the Parmesan, ground pecans, oregano, onion powder, and salt and pepper in another bowl.
4. Roll in the chicken in the egg mixture, then in the pecan mixture.
5. Put inside the microwave on high power for about 2 minutes.
6. Finish by topping with coronate, tapenade, or pesto.

Crab Cakes

Ingredients:

- Fine sea salt
- ½ teaspoon ground cumin
- ½ finely diced red bell pepper
- ½ teaspoon garlic powder
- ¼ finely chopped yellow onion
- ¼ cup ground walnuts
- ¼ cup ground flaxseeds
- Tartar sauce
- Baby spinach or mixed salad greens
- 2 tablespoons extravirgin olive oil
- 2 tablespoons finely minced fresh green chili pepper

- 1½ teaspoons curry powder

- 1 large egg

- 1 drained and flaked can crabmeat,

- 1 teaspoon onion powder

Directions:

1. Preheat the oven to 165°C. Line a foil with baking sheet. Put the oil on a skillet and heat it over medium heat.
2. Add the onion, bell pepper, and chili pepper and cook it for 4 up to 5 minutes until tender. Let it sit to slightly cool down.
3. Put the vegetables to a bowl. Mix in the egg, walnuts, cumin, curry powder, and sea salt. Combine the crabmeat and the mixture and stir well.
4. Create four patties and put it on the baking sheet. Mix together the onion powder, ground flaxseed, and garlic powder in a bowl.

5. Sprinkle the breading over your crab cakes. Bake it for about 25 minutes until it turns golden browned.
6. Serve with spinach or salad greens and tartar sauce depending on your preference.

Potato Salad With Peas And Green Beans

Ingredients:

- 100g watercress, washed

- 50g pea shoots (or baby spinach)

- 1 bunch radish, sliced in fine strips

- 1 tsp of fresh lemon juice, preferably extracted from ½ largesized lemon

- 2 tbsp flax oil

- 58 pcs mint leaves, finely chopped

- Water

- Salt and pepper to season

- 500g baby new potatoes (or marble potatoes), sliced into halves

- 200g green beans, topped and tailed

- 100g garden peas, fresh or frozen

Directions:

1. Put the halved potatoes in a saucepan with cold water, and bring to a boil. Let simmer for 10 minutes, or until potatoes are tender.
2. Drain and place potatoes in a serving bowl, and season with salt and ground black pepper.
3. Boil another 23 cups of water to a boil, add the beans and let simmer for 90 seconds. Add the peas, and let simmer for another 90 seconds.
4. Drain and add to the potatoes.
5. Add the watercress, pea shoots (or spinach), and radishes.
6. In a separate bowl, whisk the lemon juice, flax oil and finely chopped mint.
7. Season with black pepper. Pour the mixture over the salad. Toss and serve. This makes 23 servings.

Asparagus And Avocado Salad

Ingredients:

- 1 pc cucumber, sliced
- ½ pc avocado, sliced
- 2 sprigs of asparagus
- 2 bunches or handfuls of mixed salad greens, fresh or frozen, sliced
- 1 pc tomato, sliced

Directions:

1. In a bowl, place salad greens, tomato and cucumber. Mix lightly.
2. Top with avocado and asparagus. Toss, then serve.

Goat Cheese And Roast Tomatoes Stuffed Portobello Mushrooms

Ingredients:

- 1 garlic clove (enormous), finely chopped
- 4 ounces goat cheddar (plain)
- 1 tbsp. new cleaved chives
- 1 tbsp. new cleaved parsley
- Oven cooked tomatoes
- Salt and pepper
- 4 Portobello mushrooms, around 4 inches across
- 3 tbsp. olive oil
- 2 tsp. shallot, finely cleaved (This is optional.
- 1 tbsp. lemon juice

Directions:

1. Clean the Portobello mushrooms by cleaning the external piece of the covers gently, using a moist paper towel, or forget about any soil utilizing a delicate brush.
2. Take out the stems by pushing them starting with one side then onto the next until they snap off.
3. Utilizing a teaspoon, scratch the gills of the mushroom until the part under the mushroom is clean.
4. Place the mushrooms on rimmed baking sheet with a foil lining.
5. Mix lemon juice, garlic, shallot, and olive oil together. Brush the mushroom covers all around with the combination.
6. You should then sprinkle each cap with pepper and salt.

7. Preheat the grill. Make certain to put the stove rack fair and square underneath the top level.
8. Broil the mushrooms for around 3 to 5 minutes until the edges begin to brown and the mushrooms become hot. Notice that they will become delicious and delivery moisture.
9. Remove mushrooms from the oven.
10. Preheat broiler to 375 degrees Fahrenheit. In the interim, fill the mushroom covers with simmered tomatoes and speck them with goat cheddar. Sprinkle them with new herbs.
11. Bake the mushrooms for 12 minutes or until the cheddar has mellowed. You can brush the edges of the covers with additional olive oil to make them shinier and serve.

Healthy Gourmet Goulash

Ingredients:

- 1 onion (huge), chopped

- 2 15ounce jars of your beloved beans (You can utilize kidney and garbanzo beans)

- 1 garlic clove, minced

- 1 teaspoon every one of paprika and oregano

- Salt and pepper

- 1 cup elbow noodles (without gluten: rice noodles are my favorite)

- 1 pound ground hamburger (For a vegetarian rendition, you can exclude this by adding extra vegetables.)

- 2 cups diced tomatoes (some utilization the canned variety)

- 2 carrots, chopped

- 2 zucchinis, chopped

Directions:

1. Cook ground meat and the hacked onion in a skillet over medium hotness. While doing this, you can cook the elbow noodles as indicated by the guidelines on the package.
2. Mix the cooked noodles, beans, cleaved vegetables, and flavors in a major pan. You can then add the onion and meat mixture.
3. Let everything stew on mediumlow hotness for around 20 minutes or until the carrots become soft.
4. Enjoy your lunch!

Magically Wheat Free Cereal

Ingredients:

- 1/2 cup chocolate chips
- 1/2 cup vegetable oil
- 1/4 cup brown sugar
- 1/4 cup white sugar
- 2 teaspoons cinnamon
- 2 cups rolled oats
- 1/2 cup almond butter

Directions:

1. Preheat your oven to 300 degrees F. Melt the almond butter in the oil on the stovetop, then add in the sugars and cinnamon.
2. Pour the oats into a 9 x 13 inch baking sheet, then drizzle the liquid mixture over the top.

Stir until everything is damp, and place in oven.
3. Bake for 30 minutes, stirring every 10 minutes, and adding in the chocolate chips for the last 10 minutes. Cool and serve with 1 cup of skim milk.
4. Low calorie and high protein, this cereal will energize you all morning long, without adding bulk or calories to your diet.

Eiffel Tower Toast

Ingredients:

- 1 tablespoon cinnamon
- 1 tablespoon butter
- 2 slices potato flour bread
- 1 egg
- 1/4 cup skim milk

Directions:

1. Beat the eggs with the skim milk in a pie plate, and add the cinnamon. Heat a skillet on the stove over medium high heat, and add the butter.
2. Once the butter is melted, dip the bread in the eggs, coating both sides, and place them in the skillet

3. . Let the eggs cook completely and the bread toast, serve.
4. Syrup, butter, jams, and whipped topping are all great garnishes for this wheat free taste of France!
5. Filling and delicious, this breakfast will carry you away as you kick off a day off healthy eating.

Toad In A Hole Meat Version

Ingredients:

- 1 tbsp. butter

- Salt and pepper

- 2 large eggs

- 2 sausage patties, (actually you have a choice on the kind of patty to use, make some beforehand, if you want) thaw it if they're still frozen

Directions:

1. Using a knife, cut a hole in the patty. This is where you're going to have the egg, so choose the diameter as you want.
2. Heat the butter on a nonstick pan and fry the patties until it is brown on both sides.
3. Make sure that it lies flat on the pan.

4. Crack the eggs into the holes on the patties (if you wanted a scrambled version, beat the eggs with the salt and pepper before pouring them into the hole).
5. Allow the white to set completely for around 2 minutes.
6. Season with salt and pepper. Quickly flip the patties to heat the other side of the egginpatty pieces.
7. After a few seconds, slide into a plate and serve immediately.

Sausage And Ham Roll

Ingredients:

- 16 oz. cheese sauce
- 15 pieces of ham slices
- 12 oz. spicy pork sausage, ground
- 12 oz. pork sausage, ground

Directions:

1. Mix and cook the ground sausages in a large skillet over medium high flame until slightly brown.
2. Drain the sausage and mix in the cheese sauce.
3. Spoon some of the ground sausage mixture into a slice of ham and roll it up, securing it with a toothpick.

4. Fry the rolls until the ham are wellcooked. Arrange on a plate and serve with some dip or poured with sauce.

Pumpkin And Walnut Muffins

Ingredients:

- ¼ cup of honey

- 1 tsp of baking powder

- 1 tsp of cinnamon

- ½ tsp of pumpkin pie spice

- ¼ tsp of salt

- ¾ cup of chopped walnuts

- 1 cup of almond flour

- 1 cup of canned pumpkin

- 2 pcs of eggs

- ¼ cup of almond butter

Directions:

1. Turn on the oven and set it to 350°F.

2. In a large mixing bowl, combine the almond flour, pumpkin, eggs, almond butter, honey, baking powder, cinnamon, pumpkin pie spice, salt, and walnuts.
3. Stir the Ingredients: until well mixed.
4. Prepare a muffin tin and lightly grease it with cooking spray or use muffin liners. Divide the batter into six equal cups of muffin and pour it into the muffin tin.
5. Place the muffin tin inside the oven and bake for 32 to 35 minutes.
6. Once cooked, place the muffins on a wire rack to let them cool before serving.

Blueberry Muffins

Ingredients:

- 1/3 cup of coconut oil, already melted
- ½ tsp of baking soda
- ½ tsp of baking powder

- ¼ tsp of sea salt

- A pinch of cinnamon

- ½ cup of fresh blueberries

- 1 cup of almond butter

- 1 cup of almond flour

- 3 pcs of eggs, already whisked

- ½ cup of raw honey

- 1/3 cup of shredded coconut

Directions:

1. Turn on the oven and set it to 350°F.
2. In a large mixing bowl, add in the almond butter, almond flour, whisked eggs, raw honey, shredded coconut, virgin coconut oil, baking soda, baking powder, sea salt, cinnamon, and blueberries.

3. Stir the Ingredients: together until well mixed.
4. Prepare a muffin tin and line it with paper liners. Divide the batter into 8 to 10 muffin cups and pour it in the muffin tin.
5. Place the muffin tin inside the oven and bake for 15 to 20 minutes. Let the muffins cool before serving.

Peach Coconut Muffins

Ingredients:

- ¼ tsp of salt
- 2 pcs of eggs
- ¼ cup of melted coconut oil
- Half of a banana, already mashed
- ¼ cup of unsweetened applesauce
- ½ tsp of vanilla extract

- 2/3 cup of peeled and diced peaches
- 1 ½ cups of almond flour
- ¼ cup of coconut flour
- ¼ cup of unsweetened shredded coconut flakes
- 1 tsp of cinnamon
- ½ tsp of baking soda

Directions:

1. Turn on the oven and set it to 350°F.
2. Prepare a muffin tin and lightly grease it with cooking oil or line it with muffin cups.
3. In a large mixing bowl, combine the almond and coconut flour, coconut flakes, ground cinnamon, baking soda, salt, eggs, coconut oil, mashed banana, applesauce, vanilla extract, and peaches.

4. Stir the Ingredients: together until they form a smooth batter.
5. Pour the batter into the muffin tin, filling the cups about ¾ of the way. You can top each muffin with extra diced peaches if you like.
6. Place the muffin tin inside the oven and bake for 25 minutes. Once cooked, transfer the muffins into a cooling rack to cool completely.

Thai Style Beef Salad

Ingredients:

- 1 bell pepper, red
- 1 bell pepper, green
- ½ c. red onion
- 6 c. Boston lettuce
- ½ c. cucumber slices
- ½ c. torn mint leaves
- ½ c. cilantro leaves
- ¼ tsp. salt
- 12 oz. beef sirloin
- ¼ tsp. ground pepper
- 3 Tbsp. fish sauce
- ¼ c. lime juice

- 2 tsp. sugar
- 1 tsp. red pepper
- 1 garlic clove
- 1 ripe melon

Directions:

1. For this recipe, you will want to turn the grill on to heat up.
2. While the grill is heating up, you can sprinkle your steak with the pepper and salt before placing onto the grill and letting it cook for around 5 minutes on each side.
3. Move the steak to a cutting board before letting stand 5 minutes.
4. After this time, you can slice it up.
5. Meanwhile, bring out a bowl and whisk together the red pepper, garlic, sugar, fish sauce, and lime juice.

6. Cut the melon into slices so that you get 4 cups. Also, cut up the bell peppers before combining these two Ingredients: in a bowl with the mint, cilantro, cucumber, onion, and lettuce.
7. Add your beef in to the salad next before pouring the dressing on top, tossing to combine, and enjoy.

Melon Chilled Soup

Ingredients:

- ½ c. orange juice
- 1 strip orange zest
- 1 tsp. chopped ginger
- ½ c. orange juice
- ½ tsp. salt
- 6 tsp. yogurt
- 2 Tbsp. chopped cilantro
- ½ c. seedless cucumber
- 6 c. cubed melon
- 6 Tbsp. lime juice
- 1 pepper, jalapeno
- 1 Tbsp. scallion green

- 1 c. water

Directions:

1. Dice up the melon so that you get about 1 cup before combining it into a bowl with the scallion greens, 2 tablespoons of the lime juice and the cucumber.
2. Cover all of this up and let it refrigerate until ready to serve.
3. Take the rest of the lime juice and melon and place them into the blender.
4. Seed the jalapeno and cut up the scallion before adding into the blender with the salt, ginger, orange juice, orange zest, and water.
5. Blend these Ingredients: so they become smooth.
6. Refrigerate until the soup becomes chilled, which will take about 2 hours.
7. Stir the diced melon in with the rest of the mixture and divide between 4 bowls. Garnish with the yogurt and cilantro before serving.

Lemon And Rosemary Teacakes | 243 Calories

Ingredients:

- Rosemary 1 tablespoon (finely chopped)
- Almond flour 1 cup
- Arrowroot starch ¼ cup
- Baking soda ½ teaspoon
- Salt ¼ teaspoon
- Almonds sliced, for sprinkling
- Eggs 2 (separated)
- Honey ¼ cup
- Olive oil ¼ cup
- Lemon zest 1 tablespoon (fresh)

Directions:

1. In a small bowl mix beat egg whites to soft peaks and set aside.
2. In another small saucepan, melt honey and oil together; add lemon zest, rosemary and egg yolks and combine well.
3. In a medium bowl mix together almond flour, arrowroot, baking soda and salt.
4. Add almond flour mass to the oil and honey mixture to form a thick batter.
5. Add the egg white into the mass until thoroughly incorporated and mass is a pale golden.
6. Pout the mass with spoon among the greased muffin cups and sprinkle tops with almonds.
7. Bake for 1015 minutes at 200°c until teacakes are golden brown
8. Cool completely before removing from pan.

Marzipan Cake|304 Calories

Ingredients:

- Sugar 1 cup
- Almond extract 2 teaspoon
- Almond flour 2 cups
- Coconut ½ cup (shredded)
- Baking powder 1 teaspoon
- Salt ¼ teaspoon
- Butter ¼ cup
- Eggs – 3
- Olive oil ¼ cup
- Lime juice ½
- Milk ¼ cup

- Lime grated rind – 1

Directions:

1. Warm butter and olive oil, blend together and add remaining liquid Ingredients: and blend.
2. Whisk in dry Ingredients:.
3. Pour batter into greased almond cake pan and bake for about 30 minutes at 180°c and then piece of foil loosely on top.
4. Leave into the oven for another 25 minutes.
5. Cool in pan; then remove and sprinkle with powdered sugar.

Oven Baked Hot Wings

Ingredients:

- Garlic Powder: 1 teaspoon
- Green Taco Sauce: 1/4 cup
- Hot Pepper Sauce: 1/4 cup

- Sea Salt: 1/2 teaspoon

- Butter: 1/2 cup

- Cayenne Pepper: 1/2 teaspoon

- Chicken wings: 12 full wings (or 24 combined drumettes and wingettes)

- Coconut Flour: 3/4 cup

Directions:

1. Combine coconut flour, cayenne pepper, garlic powder, and salt in a large plastic container with a lid (or gallon sized zip lock bag).
2. Shake well to mix. Add chicken wings and shake well to coat
3. Remove wings from container and place on a foil lined baking sheet, chill in refrigerator for 20 minutes.
4. Heat oven to 400°.

5. Melt butter in a sauce pan, when melted whisk in hot pepper sauce and green taco sauce.
6. Remove Chicken from fridge and dip in butter sauce, returning to baking sheet.
7. Place on center rack in the oven and cook until chicken is done, about 45 minutes. Turn over once, half way through cooking time.

Veggie Wheatfree Pasta

Ingredients:

- Quinoa Macaroni Noodles: 8 ounces (1 package)
- Red Bell Pepper: 1 medium cored and sliced.
- Sea Salt: 1/4 teaspoon
- Yellow Sweet Corn: 1 cup kernels
- Parmesan Cheese: 1 ounce, freshly grated
- Black Pepper: 1/2 teaspoon
- Cherry Tomatoes: 1 cup, cut in half
- Cilantro: 2 tablespoons, chopped
- Garlic: 2 cloves, sliced
- Green Beans: 2 cups, trimmed and cut in half

- Green Onion: 1 cup, chopped

- Lemon Juice: 2 tablespoons

- Olive Oil: 1/4 cup

Directions:

1. Bring a large pot of water to boil, add corn and green beans, and cook until tender, about 35 minutes.
2. Remove corn and beans with a slotted spoon.
3. Return water to boil and add Quinoa macaroni, cook for 1012 minutes, stirring occasionally. Drain.
4. While pasta is boiling, heat 3 tablespoons of olive oil in a skillet over medium heat, add green onions, garlic, red bell pepper, and tomatoes to skillet and cook, stirring frequently for 4 minutes.
5. Toss pasta with 1 tablespoon of olive oil in a large glass bowl. Add skillet mixture, corn, and

green beans, salt, pepper, cilantro and lemon juice.
6. Toss together and serve with freshly grated parmesan cheese.

Almond Strawberry Yogurt

Ingredients:

- ¼ cup strawberries, stems removed

- Slice almonds, toasted

- ½ cup plain Greek yogurt

- 1 Tbsp. almond syrup, sugarfree

Directions:

1. Cut the esteemed strawberries into thin slices. Set to the side for the moment.
2. Mix the Greek yogurt with the almond syrup until thoroughly combined.
3. Top with the sliced strawberries and almonds and serve immediately.

Flaxseed Breakfast Wrap

Ingredients:

- 1 Tbsp. coconut oil, melted
- 1 Tbsp. water
- ¼ tsp. baking powder
- 3 Tbsp. flaxseed, ground
- 1 egg, large

Directions:

1. Shift the baking powder and flaxseed together.
2. Stir in the melted coconut oil until smooth.
3. Mix the water and egg together until smooth.
4. Combine this mixture with the mixture from Step 1 until well combined.
5. Pour the mixture onto a microwavesafe plate and microwave for 3 minutes.
6. This is the wrap.

7. Let the wrap cool for a few minutes before carefully removing it from the plate.
8. Fill the wrap with scramble eggs, fruit or sausage before rolling it up.

Roasted Squash Soup

Ingredients:

- Salt and pepper as per taste
- 6 cups chicken broth
- 1 tbsp. raisins
- 4 pounds butternut squash, in chunks
- 4 large apples
- ¼ cup olive oil

Directions:

1. Preheat oven to 450° F.
2. Take a large bowl, mix squash, apples, olive oil, salt and pepper. Spread equally on a large baking sheet. Roast for 30 minutes.
3. Continue roasting until tender and turning to brown, 15 to 20 minutes.

4. Transfer about onethird of the squash and apples in a blender with 2 cups broth.
5. Blend to smooth puree. Repeat this for remaining mixture.
6. Season with salt and heat through over medium heat, stirring continually, for about 6 minutes.
7. Serve each portion topped with raisins.

Stuffed Tomatoes

Ingredients:

- Salt and pepper, to taste
- 2 teaspoons sliced fresh chives
- 4 plum tomatoes, halved
- 1/4 cup chicken salad

Directions:

1. Scoop out insides of tomatoes with a melon biller.
2. Stuff the tomatoes with chicken salad.
3. You can bake them briefly if desired or leave as is.
4. Sprinkle with pepper and chives and enjoy.

Shrimp Skewers

Ingredients:

- 1/2 cup cilantro leaves
- 1 tbsp. garlic paste
- salt , pepper to taste 2 ½ tbsp. olive oil
- ¼ cup butter at room temperature
- 1 ½ tbsp. lemon juice
- 2 tbsp. mustard
- 3 pounds raw shrimps

Directions:

1. In a flat bowl, combine olive oil and butter.
2. Add mustard, cilantro, Lemon juice and garlic paste, salt and pepper.

3. Mix peeled and deveined shrimp and cover them thoroughly. Cover the bowl and refrigerate 1 hour.
4. Heat barbecue Grill, set it to high heat.
5. Take shrimps out of the marinade and place on skewers.
6. Brush oil the grill, and arrange shrimp skewers on it.
7. Cook for 5 minutes until well done.
8. Transfer skewers on a serving plate and enjoy.

Simple Blueberry Pancakes

Ingredients:

- A pinch of salt
- 1 ¼ cups whole wheat flour
- 2 tsp baking powder
- 1 egg
- 1 tbsp artificial sweetener
- ½ cup blueberries
- 1 cup milk, plus more if necessary

Directions:

1. Sift flour and baking powder into a mixing bowl. Stir and leave to rest.
2. In a different bowl, combine salt, artificial sweetener, egg and milk.

3. Gradually incorporate the sifted flour, until a slightly wet mixture is produced. Add the blueberries and stir once more.
4. Grease a nonstick iron skillet with lowcalorie cooking spray, or another method of your choice.
5. Place the skillet on medium heat and allow to warm for 34 minutes.
6. Spoon ¼ cup of pancake batter onto the skillet. Fry until the surface gently bubbles, then flip. Cook for 12 minutes on the other side.
7. Repeat this process until all the pancake batter has been used.
8. Serve immediately.

Cod With Herbs

Ingredients:

- ½ tsp Italian seasoning
- A pinch of garlic powder
- A pinch of black pepper
- 3 oz cod fillets
- ¼ cup fine dry bread crumbs
- 2 tbsp grated Parmesan cheese
- 1 tbsp cornmeal
- 1 tsp olive oil
- 1 egg white, lightly beaten

Directions:

1. Preheat oven to 450F.

2. In a mixing bowl combine the breadcrumbs, oil, garlic powder, pepper, cornmeal and cheese. Set aside for later.
3. Grease a broiling pan with a rack using a lowcalorie cooking spray (or another method of your choice).
4. Rest the cod on the rack and coat with a gloss of egg white.
5. Next dust the breadcrumb mixture on the salmon fillets.
6. Bake for 1214 minutes, or until the salmon breaks under gentle pressure.

Mixed Bean Stew

Ingredients:

- 2 teaspoon of oregano
- 1 tablespoon of sugar
- 1 tablespoon sunflower oil
- 8 chipolatas
- 800g mixed beans
- 800g chopped tomatoes
- 1 teaspoon of basil

Directions:

1. Heat the sunflower oil in a frying pan and fry the chipolatas for 5 minutes or until each sausage has browned on both sides.
2. Turn your slow cooker to a low setting and place the chipolatas within.

3. Add in the chopped tomatoes, mixed beans as well as the oregano, basil and sugar.
4. Leave to slow cook for 2 hours and serve.

Slow Cooked Chili Con Carne

Ingredients:

- 2 teaspoon of cumin
- 2 teaspoon of oregano
- 1kg lean minced beef
- 2 beef stock cubes
- 2 large red peppers
- 10 sundried tomatoes
- 1200g kidney beans
- 2 tablespoons of olive oil
- 2 onions
- 3 garlic cloves
- 2 tablespoons of chili powder

Directions:

1. Peel and dice the onions and chop the garlic in fine pieces.
2. In a large frying pan heat a tablespoon of the olive oil and fry the onions for 5 minutes or until soft and golden.
3. Add the garlic, oregano, cumin and chili powder and fry for an additional 2 minutes. Next, add the mince to the frying pan, frying for 15 minutes or until the mince is browned all over.
4. Add the chopped tomatoes, as well as the stock cubes and ½ a cup of water.
5. Stir thoroughly and leave to simmer for 5 minutes.
6. Turn your slow cooker on to a low setting and transfer your frying pan mixture to your slow cooker. Cover and leave to cook for 30 minutes.

7. Dice and deseed the peppers. Add the peppers and sun dried tomatoes to the slow cooker and cook for an additional 30 minutes.
8. Finally, add the kidney beans to the slow cooker and cook for an additional 20 minutes.
9. Separate into four portions and serve with a side of your choice.

Zucchini With Baby Bella Mushrooms

Ingredients:

- 2 tablespoons finely chopped fresh basil
- 1 pound zucchini
- 1 cup tomato sauce
- ¼ cup grated Parmesan cheese
- Salt and ground black pepper
- 10 sliced cremini mushrooms or baby bella
- 8 ounces uncured ground beef, sausage, chicken, turkey, or pork
- 4 tablespoons virgin olive oil
- 3 minced garlic cloves

Directions:

1. Peel the zucchini using your vegetable peeler.

2. Cut the zucchini from end to end into ribbons with your peeler up until you reach the seed core.
3. If you are going to use the meat: Heat a tablespoon of the oil in a skillet. Cook the meat. Draw off the fat.
4. Add about 2 tablespoons of oil on the skillet together with the garlic and mushroom. Cook for about 2 to 3 minutes until the mushrooms soften.
5. But if you are not going to use meat, heat 2 tablespoons oil in a skillet on medium heat. Add the garlic and mushrooms for about 2 to 3 minutes to cook.

Turkeyavocado Wraps

Ingredients:

- 2 thin slices Swiss cheese

- 1 tablespoon mustard, mayonnaise, sugarfree salad dressing, or wasabi mayonnaise

- ¼cup bean sprouts

- Flaxseed Wrap

- Handful of shredded lettuce or baby spinach leaves

- 4 deli slices roast turkey

- ½thinly sliced Hass avocado

Directions:

1. Put the Swiss cheese and turkey in the center of your flaxseed wrap. Spread the avocado, bean sprouts, and lettuce or spinach on top.

2. Top with a blob of mustard, mayonnaise, sugarfree salad dressing, wasabi mayonnaise, or any condiments of your choice then roll up.

Grilled Pear Salad With Walnut And Pomegranate Vinaigrette

Ingredients:

- 1 tablespoon honey

- 1 tablespoon glutenfree stoneground mustard

- 1 bunch watercress, trimmed

- 1 head Belgian endive, cored and thinly sliced

- ½toasted and chopped cups walnuts

- ¼tablespoon salt

- 4 tablespoons glutenfree gorgonzola cheese or crumbled blue

- 2 quartered and cored pears

- 2 tablespoons unsweetened pomegranate juice

- 1 tablespoon white wine vinegar
- 1 tablespoon olive oil

Directions:

1. Cover a nonstick grill pan or grill rack with cooking spray and heat up to medium heat. Coat the pears lightly using cooking spray.
2. Put it on the grill pan or rack for about 3 minutes on both sides until it is tender and wellmarked. Place the pears onto a plate.
3. Beat the vinegar, pomegranate juice, oil, mustard, honey, and salt together in a bowl until mixed.
4. Add the endive and watercress and put to coat equally. Top with pear wedges, 2 tablespoons of the walnuts, and a tablespoon of the cheese.

Creamy Cauliflower Salad

Ingredients:

- 1 pc red apple, chopped
- 5 tbsp mayonnaise, lowfat option
- 2 tbsp cider vinegar
- 1 pc shallot, finely chopped
- 3 cups cauliflower florets, chopped
- 2 cups romaine, heart part, chopped
- ¼ tsp ground pepper

Directions:

1. In a large bowl, whisk mayonnaise, vinegar, shallot, and ground pepper, until smooth.
2. Add in cauliflower florets, romaine, and apple slices. Toss. This makes 56 servings.

Vegetable Stirfry

Ingredients:

- ½ tray sugar snap peas
- 1 pc small ginger, chopped
- ½ clove garlic, crushed
- 1 tsp coconut butter
- ¾ tsp Tamari sauce
- ½ head broccoli, chopped
- ½ pc fennel, sliced
- 1 pc courgette, sliced
- Some coriander, chopped

Directions:

1. Fry ginger and garlic on coconut butter until lightly brown.

2. Add broccoli, fennel, courgette and sugar snap peas.
3. Add Tamari sauce and a little water. Fry while stirring and letting the vegetable steam through.
4. Remove from fire, top with chopped coriander as garnishing.
5. Serve with rice. This makes 34 servings.

Chicken With Prunes And Green Olives

Ingredients:

- ¼ cup red wine vinegar
- ¼ cup green olives, pitted and chopped
- ¼ cup prunes or dried plums, pitted and chopped
- 1 pc ¼pound chicken thighs, trimmed of fat, deboned and skinned
- 1 tsp extra virgin olive oil
- 1 cup chicken broth, low to no salt
- Ground pepper to taste

Directions:

1. Clean and rinse chicken, and pat dry with a paper towel.

2. Heat olive oil in a large nonstick pan or skillet over medium to high heat.
3. Cook chicken in oil, 2 minutes per side, until brown.
4. Add chicken broth and vinegar, and bring to a simmer while stirring constantly.
5. Add olives, prunes and some pepper. Put heat to low.
6. Cook for 12 to 15 minutes, or until chicken is no longer pink in the middle.
7. Transfer chicken to a large plate, and serve. This makes 4 servings.
8. Meats such as beef, pork, chicken, fish, and other types of seafood, are generally wheatfree.
9. Avoid adding breading to them, since most breading mixes contain flour or wheat.
10. The same is true for processed meat products such as burger patties, hotdogs, and sausages.

11. Other easy and quick to prepare options: steamed carrots, steamed green beans, baked sweet potato, steamed broccoli spears, and steamed cauliflower.

Honeylime Chicken Skewers Key West Style

Ingredients:

- 2 tablespoons honey
- Juice from one lime
- 1 to 2 teaspoons Strachan
- 2 minced garlic cloves
- 1 pound skinless and boneless chicken breasts
- 2 tablespoons cilantro
- 3 tablespoons soy sauce (check to ensure it is wheat free)
- 1 tablespoon coconut oil
- Red pepper drops, to taste

Directions:

1. In a little bowl, blend all fixings with the exception of the chicken. Make certain to join everything thoroughly.
2. Pour the marinade over the chicken bosoms and go to cover them completely. Cover and permit the marinade to absorb for no less than an hour.
3. Grill the chicken on medium high hotness for 68 minutes for each side. You will realize when it's done when the juices run clear.

Mushroom Risotto

Ingredients:

- 2 tablespoons olive oil

- 7 ounces grams grouped mushrooms, sliced

- 750 ml sans wheat or sans gluten vegetable stock

- 2 teaspoons dried oregano

- 1.7 ounces of parmesan cheddar, ground (for vegetarian adaptation, discard this or use sans dairy parmesan)

- Additional bubbling water

- 7 ounces risotto rice (Arborio)

- 1 onion, chopped

- 1 green pepper, chopped

- 1 red pepper, chopped

- Freshly ground dark pepper

Directions:

1. In a weighty lined skillet, put 2 tablespoon olive oil or coconut oil and add the rice.
2. Delicately heat the rice for around 23 minutes, until the rice looks translucent.
3. Add the onion, mushrooms, and peppers, and cook for an additional 5 minutes. Be mindful so as not to brown the rice.
4. Add vegetable stock and heat to the point of boiling. Lessen the hotness and stew the rice for around 25 minutes.
5. Add bubbling water as important, to ensure that the combination doesn't dry out.
6. When cooking is done, the risotto ought to be soggy, delicate, and rich, not dry. It is smarter to leave the risotto somewhat wetter than concoct a dry one.

Add the oregano and dark pepper. Blend well.
7. Serve with ground parmesan on top, or for a vegetarian rendition, with sans dairy parmesan.

Eggy Booster

Ingredients:

- 2 finely chopped green onions
- ½ cup shredded cheese
- 1/2 small can chopped mushrooms, drained
- 3 eggs
- 1/2 cup skim milk
- 1/4 cup chopped tofu
- 1 small fresh tomato, chopped

Directions:

1. Spray a medium skillet with no stick spray and heat on medium high heat. Mix all Ingredients: except for the cheese in a mixing bowl.

2. Add to the heated skillet, and cook slowly, stirring often to prevent sticking or burning. Garnish with the cheese and serve.
3. Tofu is an easy and delicious way to add protein to a dish without compromising flavor or calories.

Delicious Potato And Egg Party

Ingredients:

- 2 tablespoons olive oil

- Salt and pepper to taste

- 1/4 small white onion, chopped

- 2 boiled eggs, coined

- 8 stalks asparagus, cut in half lengthwise

- 1 baked potato, cubed

Directions:

1. Heat the oil in a skillet on medium high heat, add in all vegetables, and sauté until the onions are tender, this will be about 8 to 10 minutes. Sprinkle on salt and pepper to suit your taste. Enjoy!
2. Asparagus is a delicious way to get nutrition into your diet, but keep the calories out.

Greek Souvlaki

Ingredients:

- 1 lb. lamb meat, shoulder part
- 2 tbsp. lemon juice
- ¼ cup olive oil
- 1 tsp. garlic, minced
- 1 tsp. dried oregano, Greek

Directions:

1. Cut the meat into cubes, minimizing the included fat. Combine the rest of the Ingredients: as marinade.
2. Place the meat cubes into the mixture and marinate in the fridge for at least 4 hours, but not too long.

3. Set grill to medium high heat. Cook meat for 8 to 10 minutes, depending on your preference. Be careful not to overcook.

Chicken Salad With Peas

Ingredients:

- 1/3 cup mayonnaise

- ¼ cup scallions or green onions, sliced

- 2 cups cooked chicken, diced

- ½ cup olives (or as much as you prefer)

- 3 tbsp. basil

- ½ cup frozen green peas

Directions:

1. Thaw the peas and drain in colander.
2. Dice chicken and place them in a bowl, add in the halved olives and the sliced green onions.
3. Paper towel dry the peas and mix in with the others.

4. In a separate bowl, whisk mayonnaise with pesto. Fold into the salad and chill for 12 hours before serving.

Irish Soda Bread

Ingredients:

- ½ cup of raisins

- 2 pcs of eggs

- 2 tbsp of agave nectar

- 2 tbsp of apple cider vinegar

- 2 ¾ cups of blanched almond flour

- ¼ tsp of Celtic sea salt

- 1 ½ tsp of baking soda

- A pinch of caraway seeds

Directions:

1. In a large mixing bowl, add in the almond flour, baking soda, Celtic sea salt, and raisins. Stir the Ingredients: to combine.

2. Add in the eggs, apple cider vinegar, and agave nectar into the bowl. Mix the Ingredients: together until properly combined.
3. Place the dough over a piece of parchment paper. Use a rolling pin to form the dough into an 8in circle that is 1 ½in thick.
4. Score the top of the dough about ½in deep in the shape of a cross using a serrated knife. Sprinkle the caraway seeds evenly on the top of the dough.
5. Prepare a baking sheet and place the dough with the parchment paper on it. Place the baking sheet in the oven and bake for 20 minutes at 350°F. Once baking time has elapsed, turn off the oven and leave the bread inside for 10 minutes more.
6. Remove the baking sheet in the oven and let it cool for another 30 minutes before slicing and serving.

Chocolate Zucchini Bread

Ingredients:

- 2 pcs of large eggs
- 2 tbsp of coconut oil
- ¼ cup of honey
- ¼ tsp of vanilla stevia
- 1 ¼ cups of blanched almond flour
- ¼ cup of cacao powder
- ¼ tsp of Celtic sea salt
- ½ tsp of baking soda
- ¾ cup of zucchini, already grated

Directions:

1. Add the cacao powder and almond flour in a large mixing bowl fit for a food processor. Mix the Ingredients: together.
2. Add in the Celtic sea salt and baking soda into the bowl and stir again.
3. Add in the eggs, honey, coconut oil, vanilla stevia, and zucchini. Use the food processor to mix the Ingredients:. Blend until the Ingredients: are well incorporated.
4. Prepare a 6.5" x 4" loaf pan. Lightly grease the pan using coconut oil and dust it with almond flour. Pour the batter inside the loaf pan and place it inside the oven.
5. Bake for 35 to 40 minutes at 350°F. Once done, let it cool on a wire rack for 2 hours.

Double Chocolate Chunk Cookies

Ingredients:

- ½ tsp of sea salt

- 1 stick of butter, sliced into cubes

- 1 cup of coconut sugar

- 2 pcs of large eggs

- 8 oz of bittersweet chocolate, melt the first half and coarsely chop the second half

- 1 ½ cups of almond flour

- ½ cup of unsweetened natural cocoa

- ½ tsp of baking soda

- 1 tsp of pure vanilla extract

Directions:

1. Turn on the oven and set it to 350°F.

2. In a large mixing bowl, combine the unsweetened cocoa, almond flour, salt, baking soda, and sugar. Use a hand mixer or whisk to mix the Ingredients:.
3. Add in the cubes of butter and process until they're combined with the dry Ingredients:.
4. Then, add in the eggs, vanilla extract, and melted chocolate into the bowl.
5. Blend the Ingredients: together until they becomes smooth. Stir in the chopped pieces of chocolate.
6. Prepare a baking sheet and line it with parchment paper.
7. Drop a tablespoon of cookie mixture into the baking sheet and place each drop a few inches apart.
8. Place the baking sheets inside the oven and bake for 8 to 10 minutes. Rotate the baking sheets about halfway through the baking time.

9. Bake the cookies until it has just set. Then, transfer the cookies into a wire rack and let it cool completely.

Squash Parmesan Cakes

Ingredients:

- ¼ tsp. ground pepper
- ¼ tsp. salt
- 2 c. shredded summer squash
- 1 Tbsp. olive oil
- 2/3 c. chopped shallots
- 1 egg
- 1 Tbsp. chopped parsley
- ½ c. Parmesan cheese

Directions:

1. To start this recipe you can turn on the oven and preheat it so it can reach 400 degrees.

2. While the oven is heating up you can bring out a bowl and beat the egg. Stir the pepper, salt, parsley, and shallots in as well.
3. Place the squash into a kitchen towel and then gather the ends to squeeze out the liquid.
4. Add the cheese and squash into the bowl before stirring in order to combine.
5. Next, take the oil and heat it up on a skillet. Pack about 1/3 cup of the squash mixture into a cup before unmolding it and patting down into a small cake.
6. Repeat this process to get 4 cakes. Place into the skillet and cook so they become crispy and browned, which will take around 4 minutes.
7. Turn the cakes around before placing onto a pan and into the oven. Bake for around 10 minutes before serving.

Chicken Stuffed Tomatoes

Ingredients:

- ¼ c. chicken salad
- 4 tomatoes, plum
- 2 tsp. sliced chives
- Pepper

Directions:

1. To start this recipe, you will take out a melon baller and scoop out the insides of your plum tomatoes.
2. Once the tomatoes are all cleared out, you can take the chicken salad and use it to fill up the tomatoes.
3. After the tomatoes are completely filled up, you can sprinkle on the chives and the pepper on top of everything. When ready, serve this recipe right away and enjoy!

Sausage And Mushroom Quiches

Ingredients:

- 1 tsp. pepper
- ¼ c. Swiss cheese, shredded
- 5 eggs
- 1 c. milk
- 8 oz. breakfast sausage, turkey
- 8 oz. sliced mushrooms
- 1 tsp. olive oil
- ¼ c. scallions, sliced
- 3 egg whites

Directions:

1. Take one of the racks from the oven and set it in the center. Once that it done you can turn on the oven and preheat it to 325 degrees.
2. While the oven is heating up, take a muffin tin and coat it with some cooking spray before continuing.
3. Next, grab a skillet and heat it up on the oven. Add the sausage to the skillet and let it cook for about 7 minutes so that it becomes golden brown.
4. At this time, you can transfer the sausage to a bowl and allow it some time to cool down.
5. Add some more oil to your pan before adding in the mushrooms and letting them cook so they turn golden brown, which will take about 5 minutes. Once the mushrooms are cooked, you can place them into the bowl along with the sausage to cool down.
6. After 5 minutes, add the pepper, cheese, and scallions to the bowl.

7. Bring out another bowl and whisk together the milk, egg whites, and egg.
8. Divide this mixture between your muffin tin before sprinkling on some of the sausage mixture into each cup. Try to distribute it as evenly as possible.
9. Place the muffin tin into the oven and let it cook for around 25 minutes so that the tops start to brown.
10. After it is done cooking, allow it to cool down for about 5 minutes on a wire rack before taking out of the muffin tin and letting it finish cooling down completely before enjoying.

Shrimp With Curried Rice

Ingredients:

- 1 c. white rice
- 2 tsp. curry powder
- Salt
- Pepper
- ½ c. basil
- 1 chopped onion
- 1 Tbsp. olive oil
- 2 chopped carrots
- 2 chopped garlic cloves
- 1 ½ lb. peeled shrimp

Directions:

1. To start this recipe, you can heat up a little bit of oil on a skillet.
2. Once the skillet it warmed up, you will want to add in the carrots and the onion and let them cook for about 8 minutes or until they become soft and begin to brown a little bit around the edges
3. After this time, you can add in the curry powder and the garlic to this mixture and let it cook for about 2 minutes.
4. Next, take the pepper, salt, 2 ½ cups of water, and the rice and add these Ingredients: into the skillet. Let everything come to boil.
5. Once everything reaches boil, you can reduce the heat of the skillet, cover everything up, and let the Ingredients: simmer for about 15 minutes or until soft and tender.
6. While the Ingredients: in the skillet are simmering, you can take some pepper and salt and season the shrimp with them.

7. Nestle the shrimp into the rice, cover the skillet, and let it cook for another 5 minutes so that the shrimp become opaque throughout.
8. Fold in the basil last and let it cook for a few minutes to get heated through. When you are ready, serve this dish right away and enjoy.

Apple Cake

Ingredients:

- Coconut ¼ cup (shredded)
- Cinnamon 2 teaspoons
- Coconut flour 1 cup
- Apples 3
- Sugar 1 cup
- Egg – 1
- Nuts ½ cup (chopped)
- Olive oil ¾ cup

Directions:

1. Take a small bowl, wash and cut apples into pieces and mix with 1 tablespoon of sugar, coconut and cinnamon. Stir well and place and set aside.

2. In another bowl mix flour, ¾ cup sugar, olive oil, egg and nuts together, combine well and pour over apple mixture.
3. Insert into the preheated oven at 190°c bake until the top is golden brown.

Pumpkin Pie

Ingredients:

For Pie Crust

- Cocoa powder 1 teaspoon
- Egg 1
- Butter – 100 g (melted)
- Walnuts 1 ¼ cups (ground)
- Flaxseed ¼ cup (ground)
- Ground cinnamon 1 teaspoon

For Pie Filling

- Ground cinnamon 2 teaspoons
- Ground nutmeg 1½ teaspoons
- Ground ginger 1 teaspoon
- Pumpkin puree 2 cups

- Cream cheese 250 g (softened)

- Eggs – 2

- Coconut milk ½ cup

- Vanilla extract 2 teaspoons

- Truvia 6 tablespoons

Directions:

1. Take a large bowl and combine ground walnuts, flaxseed, cinnamon and cocoa powder and mix well.
2. In another small bowl, beat eggs and add butter. Pour egg mixture into walnut mixture and combine well. Transfer the mixture into the greased pan.
3. In another bowl, combine pumpkin, cream cheese, eggs, coconut milk, and vanilla extract and combine well.
4. Add cinnamon, nutmeg, ginger and sweetener and continue stirring.
5. Pour pumpkin mixture into pie pan and bake into the preheated oven at 200°c for 40 minutes.
6. Sprinkle additional nutmeg and cinnamon and top with whipped cream or whipped coconut milk.

Wonderful Coconut Shrimp

Ingredients:

- Coconut Oil: 3 tablespoons
- Egg: 1 large, beaten
- Jumbo Shrimp (or prawns): 1 pound, peeled and deveined
- Limes: 2, zested and cut into wedges
- Cabbage: 4 cups, Shredded
- Carrots: 2 cups, Shredded
- Coconut: 1/2 cup, shredded
- Coconut Flour: 2/3 cup
- Turmeric: 2 teaspoons

Directions:

1. Heat coconut oil in a large skillet over medium heat.
2. Combine lime zest, turmeric, coconut flour and shredded coconut in a large bowl.
3. Dip shrimp in egg, dredge in coconut mixture and place in hot oil. Cook uncovered until golden brown, about 34 minutes per side.
4. Remove from heat and set on a paper towel for about 5 minutes to dry.
5. Serve over a bed of shredded cabbage and carrots, squeeze lime wedges over shrimp before serving.

Chicken Cornbread Casserole

Ingredients:

- Chicken Breast: 2, boneless, skinless, cut into strips

- Butter: 2 tablespoons

- Mild Cheddar Cheese: 1 cup, shredded

- Black Pepper: 1/2 teaspoon

- Turmeric: 1/2 teaspoon

- Basil: 1/2 teaspoon, dried

- Cornbread cubes: 4 cups, dried

- Garlic: 1 tablespoon, minced

- Sweet Onion: 1 cup, chopped

- Celery: 1/2 cup, chopped

- Low Sodium Chicken Broth: 1 can

- Milk: 1 cup

- Tapioca Flour: 2 tablespoons

- Eggs: 2 large, beaten

Directions:

1. Heat oven to 350°.
2. Melt butter in a skillet over medium heat, add chicken, and cook, turning frequently, until chicken is white, about 5 minutes.
3. Add onion, garlic and celery, cook until celery softens and onion becomes transparent, about 5 more minutes.
4. Stir together milk and tapioca flour in a small dish, pour into skillet. Add pepper, basil and turmeric.
5. Bring to a boil stirring frequently, turn down heat and simmer until the sauce begins to thicken.
6. Place cornbread cubes in a large bowl, add chicken broth, eggs, and contents of skillet.

Stir together until well mixed and the cornbread is moistened.
7. Place cornbread mixture in a 13 x 8 glass baking dish, place foil over the top and cook on center rack of oven for about 20 minutes.
8. Remove foil, sprinkle cheeses over the top and return to oven, cooking until cheese is melted, about 10 more minutes.

Simple Pancakes

Ingredients:

- 1 Tbsp. flaxseed, ground
- 3 eggs, large
- ¾ cup light milk, coconut or almond
- 2 Tbsp. olive oil, extra light
- 3 cups ground almond meal
- ½ tsp. salt
- ½ tsp. baking soda

Directions:

1. In a mixing bowl, combine the almond meal, flaxseed, salt and baking soda together. Add the eggs and whisk until well incorporated.

2. Pour the milk and oil into the mixture and whisk until smooth. Set the mixture to the side and let rest for about 5 minutes.
3. While the mixture is resting, heat a bit of oil in a skillet.
4. Make the pancakes by adding about ¼ cup of the batter to the heated skillet and letting cook for about 3 minutes. Flip the pancake over and cook on the other side for an additional 3 minutes.
5. Continue making the pancakes as stated in Step 4.
6. Serve the pancakes while still warm with fresh fruit.

Cream Of Wheat Alternative

Ingredients:

- ¼ cup golden flaxseed, ground
- Coconut milk
- Honey
- ¼ cup fruit, such as strawberries or blueberries

Directions:

1. Place the ground flaxseed in a microwave safe. Add enough coconut milk so that it barley covers the ground flaxseed.
2. Cook the mixture in the microwave for about 40 seconds. Stir in ½ to 1 tsp. of honey. Top with the fruit and enjoy.

Chicken Salad

Ingredients:

- 1 tbsp. onion (minced)
- ½ tbsp. garlic powder
- ½ avocado
- 1 tbsp. lemon juice
- 2 cups water
- 1/2 lb. boneless skinless chicken breasts
- 1 bunch celery (diced)
- 1 can tomatoes
- Salt and pepper to taste

Directions:

1. Heat a large skillet over medium heat. Add water and bring to a boil, then reduce the heat.
2. Add Chicken breasts in the water and poach for 1015 minutes.
3. Turn off heat and let the chicken sit for about 5 minutes.
4. When cool, dice it to small pieces. Cool in the refrigerator for an hour.
5. Remove from the refrigerator and add the diced celery, garlic powder, tomatoes, avocado, lemon juice, salt and pepper.
6. Serve cold on lettuce bed.

Roasted Chicken

Ingredients:

- 1/3 cup margarine, divided
- 5/8 stalk celery
- 3 pound whole chicken, giblets removed
- salt and black pepper to taste
- 2 teaspoons onion powder

Directions:

1. Preheat oven to 350o F.
2. Place chicken in a roasting pan and season generously inside and out with salt and pepper and onion powder.
3. Place 3 tablespoons margarine in the cavity of the chicken.

4. Arrange remaining margarine on outer side. Cut celery into pieces and place in the cavity of the chicken.
5. Bake for one hour and 15 minutes in oven to a internal temperature of 180 degrees F.
6. Remove from heat and sprinkle with margarine and lard. Cover with foil and let stand 30 minutes before serving.

Oriental Nutty Chicken

Ingredients:

- 2 cups white rice, uncooked
- 3 tbsp, garlic chopped
- 2 ¼ cups broccoli florets
- ½ cup unsalted dryroasted peanuts
- 3 tbsp olive oil
- 4 cups water
- 5 tsp soy sauce
- 2 tbsp peanut butter
- 1 ½ tbsp ginger root, grated
- 1 cup spring onions, chopped
- 1 ½ tsp white wine vinegar

- A pinch of cayenne peppers

- 4 chicken breasts, boneless, skinless, halved and cut into strips

Directions:

1. Bring a large saucepan of water to the boil over high heat. Throw in the rice, lower the heat and cover with a lid. Leave to simmer for 20 minutes.
2. In a mixing bowl, combine vinegar, a pinch of cayenne pepper, soy sauce and peanut butter. Leave in one place for later.
3. In a large nonstick iron skillet, warm 3 tbsp olive oil over high heat. Throw in the garlic, ginger and chicken. Cook until the chicken is golden on both sides; this should take no more than 34 minutes per side.
4. Lower the heat to a medium setting add the remaining Ingredients: and sauce made earlier. Cook until all the vegetables have

softened and the chicken is cooked throughout.
5. Serve the peanut chicken with a portion of rice.

Nutty Energy Bars

Ingredients:

- ½ tsp ground cinnamon
- ½ cup bran cereal
- ¼ cup unsalted sunflower seeds
- ¼ cup chopped walnuts
- 6 tsp brown sugar
- 2 tablespoons sunflower oil
- 1 cup quick cooking rolled oats
- 1 beaten egg
- ½ cup whole wheat flour
- ¼ cup applesauce
- ¼ cup honey

- 7oz dried mixed fruit

Directions:

1. Preheat the oven to 325F. Take a 9inch baking pan and cover it with tin foil. Next, coat the tin foil with low calorie cooking spray.
2. In a mixing bowl, combine all the dry Ingredients:. Stir together until everything is evenly distributed and add the wet Ingredients:. Stir thoroughly once more.
3. Transfer the bowl contents into the baking pan and spread it evenly.
4. Cook for 30 minutes, or until the mixture has become firm and lightly golden. Remove the cooked slab using the tin foil as leverage. Cut the bar into 12 even pieces. Keep fresh in the refrigerator.

Slow Cooked Prawn Curry

Ingredients:

- 3 tablespoons curry paste
- 400g shelled raw king prawns
- 250g frozen peas
- 1 tablespoon of vegetable oil
- 2 onions
- 6 tomatoes
- Large piece of fresh root ginger
- 6 garlic cloves
- Coriander

Directions:

1. Peel the onions. Cut the onions in half and slice each onion half into six even sized

wedges. Cut each of the tomatoes into eight wedges.

2. Peel the ginger and chop it into small pieces. Finally, cut the garlic cloves into moderate sized chunks.

3. In a frying pan, heat the vegetable oil and fry the onions for 5 minutes or until soft and golden. Remove the onion from the pan and process with the tomatoes and ginger in a food processor, leaving ¼ of the tomatoes for later usage.

4. Fry the remaining tomatoes with the curry paste for 5 minutes. Add the prawns and fry until the prawns are thoroughly cooked.

5. Transfer the content of the frying pan and food processor to your slow cooker.

6. Turn your slow cooker to a low setting, add the peas and coriander to the mix and stir. Cover and slow cook for 2 hours. Separate into four portions and serve.

Oriental Barbecued Pork

Ingredients:

- 2 garlic cloves
- Small piece of fresh ginger
- 1 teaspoon of sesame oil
- ½ teaspoon of fivespice mix
- 1 boneless pork shoulder, fat trimmed
- ¼ cup of soy sauce
- ¼ cup of hoisin sauce
- 3 tablespoons of ketchup
- 3 tablespoons of honey
- 250ml chicken broth

Directions:

1. Crush the garlic. Peel and grate the ginger. Combine the soy sauce, hoisin sauce, ketchup, honey, crushed garlic, sesame oil and five spice powder in a bowl.
2. Stir thoroughly. Transfer the spice sauce to a sealable plastic bag. Add the pork to the plastic bag, and then shake the bag and leave to marinate for 2 hours.
3. Next, place your slow cooker onto a low setting. Empty your pork and spice sauce into the slow cooker. Cover and leave for 8 hours.
4. Finally, add the chicken broth and slow cook for another 30 minutes. Tear the pork into shreds and serve alongside the sauce.

www.ingramcontent.com/pod-product-compliance
Lightning Source LLC
LaVergne TN
LVHW010219070526
838199LV00062B/4665